T5-AAP-195

Wish I May, Wish I Might

Wish I May, Wish I Might

Fantastic Thoughts for a Starry Night

Florian and Gabriele Langenscheidt

Translated from the German
by Laura Lindgren

ABBEVILLE PRESS PUBLISHERS
New York London Paris

Editor: Amy Handy
Cover designer: Celia Fuller
Interior designer: Laura Lindgren
Production director: Simone René

LIBRARY OF CONGRESS CATALOGING-IN-PUBLICATION DATA

Sternschnuppenwünsche. English.
    Wish I may, wish I might : fantastic thoughts for a
starry night / [collected by] Florian and Gabriele Langenscheidt : translated from the German by Laura Lindgren;
[illustrations, Gabriele Langenscheidt]. — 1st ed.
      p.   cm.
    ISBN 1-55859-638-0
    1. Wishes. I. Langenscheidt, Florian. II. Langen-
scheidt, Gabriele. III. Lindgren, Laura. IV. Title.
GR615.S7413   1993
838´.9140208—dc20   93-4880

Copyright © 1992 Wilhelm Heyne Verlag GmbH & Co., KG, Munich
English-language translation and compilation copyright © 1993 Abbeville Press.
Illustrations: Gabriele Langenscheidt

First edition

3   5   7   9   10   8   6   4

We have forgotten how to wish. We may make wishes on birthdays or holidays, but adulthood steals our grand dreams of a better world. An excess of reason tempers our thoughts and deeds.

But only those who believe can move mountains and only the visionary can change the world. We ought to have the courage and spirit to wish and to dream and not sink into the humdrum routine of everyday life.

Such are the thoughts that led us to the concept of this book one starry August night. We wanted to collect the wishes people make—big and small, personal and political, romantic and realistic. On this night we were in the company of a few children, and theirs were the nicest wishes of all. So in the course of gathering all these wishes together, we asked some grade-school children to add some of their wishes to our collection. Their contributions were invaluable.

Shooting stars are there to help us. They seem no bigger than your fingertip, yet their power is great. Whatever we wish the moment we see them fall will surely come to pass. It's easy—all you have to do is think of the right thing to wish under a star-filled sky.

Five billion shooting stars fall each night—one for each of the earth's inhabitants. And for those who don't believe in their power—well, there are always fairies and other magical creatures to turn to.

⬦ *Florian and Gabriele Langenscheidt* ⬦

P.S. For those who have more wishes to make and care to share them, here is space at the back to write them in. Maybe your wishes will bring someone else a little happiness.

When you see a shooting star,
make a wish . . .

to have to go to the office
only every other day.

to be transported to another time.

to make an earth-shattering discovery.

for a pet that always behaves.

to turn into a good fairy.

to spend three whole months traveling.

to sit atop a sunflower and heal
all the world's children.

to play piano like van Cliburn.

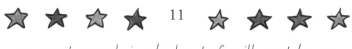

to spend a week in the land of milk and honey.

to sleep like a baby again.

that a coconut never falls on my head.
(or the sky).

to see the earth from the moon someday.

that status symbols will lose all meaning.

that my husband will finally be promoted.

to have better weather this weekend.

that it doesn't always have to be that some have no work and others have too much.

that the day comes when we don't need Amnesty International.

that there were more playgrounds, ice cream parlors, and sidewalk cafés.

that things never get so bad that no one
wants to bring a child into the world.

to slide down a rainbow.

that everybody I love stays healthy.

that my sweetheart will admit to having
made a mistake now and then too.

to win a game show just once.

that sometimes lies didn't get discovered.

that my Prince Charming
won't turn into a frog.

that I don't always have to be superman.

to have ten wishes that will
all come true.

to be invited by a fantastically handsome
young man to accompany him on his yacht
in the Caribbean.

to be so tiny that I could be the conductor
of a toy train.

to be able to draw like Picasso.

to travel around the world someday.

to do away with billboard advertisements.

to have nothing but pleasant dreams from now on.

to be able to foresee the future once in a while.

that at certain moments our
children would simply disappear
for an hour.

that the Great Lakes were filled with cream.

to find a beach with sand
that would not stick to suntan lotion.

that spaghetti made me thin.

to send a falling star to my love,
who is so far away.

that wars would only happen in history books.

that my children's lives will be truly happy.

that this book gives its readers the inspiration not to take the world for granted.

that my colleague won't consider my viewpoint with total indifference.

that my teddy bear would come to life.

that nobody has to be alone on Christmas.

that my friends, my family, and I
will all be in heaven together.

that McDonald's, Disneyworld, and
Benetton don't take over the whole world.

that the snow will turn white again.

to stay attractive my whole life without going to the gym and in spite of dining regularly at the little Italian place around the corner.

that my violin would practice all by itself.

to have a quiet moment to read the paper every morning.

that governments would treat their citizens a little more decently.

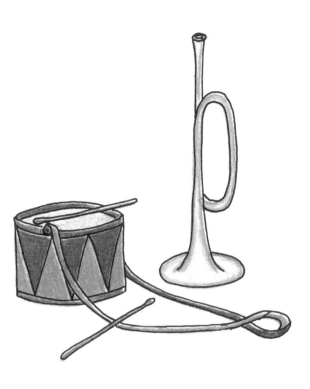

that children were allowed to be noisy.

that supermarkets won't put
all the mom-and-pop stores out of business.

that this book will be a little bestseller.

to have four more weeks of vacation every year.

that all religions would be free of hypocrisy.

that my thinking cap turns into
a funnel that knowledge pours through.

that my cat will come back home.

that the cynics aren't right
and the optimists won't die out.

that our rent would be cut in half.

that I will never feel old and lonely.

that nuclear arms will be
immediately banned all over the world.

to float on a cloud up to God
and bring my grandma back.

to be able to travel with
Jacques Cousteau for a year.

to live to be a hundred years old—
but to be mentally and physicially fit.

never to have to
clean up again.

that I could ride my bike
to the end of the rainbow.

to live in a little cottage
right in the middle of an immense garden.

to be able to talk with animals.

to have a horse with a beautiful western saddle.

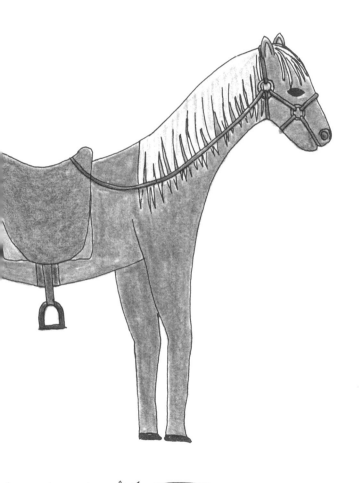

that the establishment will finally
come to appreciate individuality.

that she, that singularly irresistable creature,
will call again tonight and never want
to stop talking.

that the dentist never has to use a drill again.

that women will never again be treated unfairly.

to be able to communicate
with my children again.

that the generations to come
will still have coral reefs to marvel at.

that "he" will come to his senses.

that "she" will come to her senses.

that my children never
succumb to the influence of drugs.

to get all the presents
i'm wishing for on my birthday.

that new paths are always forged.

that never, never again
will a human being die of hunger.

that every adolescent has at least one
trustworthy friend to confide in during
those difficult years.

that she can forgive me one more time.

that someday a blimp will fly over
the Atlantic again.

that people can have a little more time
for each other.

that i'm brave enough to jump off the high-dive.

that everyone learns to read and write.

that we can start all over again.

that scientists discover that
hamburgers are good for you.

that romantics never die out.

for greater courage to go it alone.

that nobody will ever make fun
of my freckles again.

that once in a while the clock would
stand still for a couple of hours.

to remain friends if our romance
should ever come to an end.

that every day was my birthday.

that no child will ever be mistreated again.

that politics will be practiced
with greater competence and compassion.

to pass the exams with flying colors.

that my hamster will get well soon.

that there will be no more mosquitoes
that always bite only me.

that being will prevail over having.

that my children never smash into anything.

that the stupid misunderstanding we had will
at last be resolved and we can laugh about it.

that we can spend a whole night
together again.

... أن يأتي يوم يهلّ فيه السلام على الشرق
الأوسط

that Mondays will go away.

for more time to spend
with my family.

that Venice never sinks into the ocean.

that we can save our marriage.

..., чтобы Содружество Независимых Государств нашло свой путь в свободу без потерь.

that women don't have to be afraid of being in parking garages at night anymore.

to get to have dinner with Paul Bocuse.

to spend at least one night
with the girl I have a crush on.

to have a hat that makes me invisible.

never to have to go to the office.

to be able to do something so amazing
that I could perform in the circus.

to sleep for a night in a teepee.

to master a secret language.

to transform the world.

to live with Snoopy, Donald,
and the Turtles.

to have a whole roomful of stuffed animals.

that I never hurt anybody
by forgetting to thank them.

to be more receptive to
other people and their opinions.

that everybody has a friend to talk to.

that our firm's sales
go sky-high next year.

that a cure for AIDS will finally be discovered.

that the idea that we might be reincarnated
somewhere in the world a hundred years
from now is not too alarming.

for more people with the courage to have
their own opinions.

that each of us finds our own little paradise
more than once.

for enough guardian angels
for all the children of the world.

that I hadn't said that.

雲になれま
すように

that someday the poor get everything they need.

that I was a head taller.

that my chicken pox will just disappear
with the next full moon.

that the animals won't have
to freeze in the winter.

that a wonderful relationship blossoms
from this intense week-long flirtation.

that the sun shines every day.

to be really proud of my parents.

that we'll get our dream house.

that the pope stops opposing birth control.

that nobody loses hope.

that someday there will be no more armies.

that never again will an animal lose its life
for the sake of a fur coat.

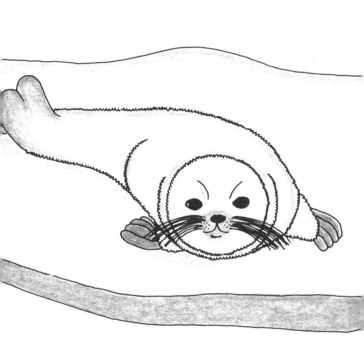

to be little again once in a while
and snuggle up in Mama's bed.

to ride on a dinosaur someday.

to spend our next vacation on a tropical island
beneath palm trees (without the kids).

to spend a night on the moon
with my best friend.

to get to eat ice cream
three times a day every day.

to be able to turn into a mouse now and then.

to plan and build my very own house.

to be seventeen again.

never to be stuck in traffic again.

that never again must a child
come into the world unwanted.

that school grades wouldn't be taken so seriously.

that 1 + 1 = 3, just once.

that men would change.

that someday equal rights will really be equal.

that money would't play
such a big role in the world.

that all the lonely people of the world
will find somebody to love.

that the sun never does us any harm.

that no adult will ever cross the street when
the light is red and children are around.

that our hearts still flutter with love even in
the autumn years of our marriage.

for my opponent's baseline on the tennis court
to move a little farther back.

that the world never stops turning.

that we never run out of wishes.

★ ★ ★ ☆ ★ ★ ★

to be able to program my VCR.

that we could just slide through telephone cables
and eliminate the distance between us.

that we wouldn't use advertising to exploit the
diversity of culture and the human race.

that I could keep my cool a little better
amid the chaos of my family.

that no two days are ever alike.

that a nuclear power plant
never blows up.

that the IRS would have to shut down
for a lack of personnel.

that our friendship will last a lifetime.

that my parents will try a little harder
to understand me.

that certain days had more than 24 hours.

to sprout wings.

that a cure for depression will be found.

that people never give up reading—in spite of
TV, videos, and computers.

to stand high atop a mountain
and reach out and touch the stars.

to have five minutes to myself more often.

to be somebody else for a little while.

to die with dignity.

to be friends again.

to have my own room.

91

to feel with all the intensity of a child.

to create something that will make me immortal.

to meet the love of my life—today!

to be a mind reader.

never to be dependent on other people.

that our kids get home safely.

that aging was not so unjustly different
for men and women.

for a white Christmas again.

that cat and mouse would get along.

that someday we suddenly notice
that there's no more terrorism.

that puberty would go away.

that Granny's eyesight will be good again.

that the man of my dreams will
finally realize that he loves me too.

that the air will again be clean enough
to breathe deeply, and the water so clean that
fish of all kinds thrive in the sea.

that the dinosaurs will live again . . .

. . . (at least in the
hearts of children).

that I would not be so very shy
when I meet strangers.

to be always young at heart.

that everybody has someone
to take care of them when they're sick.

that our hope of having a child
will be fulfilled at last.

that the whales will multiply again.

that the results of the medical tests prove
there was nothing to worry about.

to win the lottery someday.

that my life didn't seem so senseless.

that people don't completely give up
overindulging themselves once in a while.

to spend a whole weekend in a treehouse.

to meet the baby Jesus.

to play tennis much better and be able to ski.

to find an enormous treasure.

to turn into a mermaid and
frolic with the fish.

to be a child again.

to find the fountain of youth.

never to have to leave home.

106

to be more spontaneous and express
my feelings better.

for books that never end.

that we never treat our children unfairly.

that someday we'll stand
on the Eiffel tower together.

that the koala bears
won't become extinct.

to live in a lighthouse.

to visit my family more often.

to have a cellar full of chocolates and fine wine.

to be just half as funny as Groucho Marx.

that the whole world lay before my feet.

that art will never die.

for efficient ways to distribute our surplus
to the poor people of the world.

that our child, in spite of
a difficult pregnancy,
comes into the world safe and sound.

that my ailing sister will be
miraculously healed.

that our neighbors don't move away.

that tomatoes will taste like tomatoes again.

that our grandchildren will be able to swim
in all the world's rivers and lakes.

that Mommy and Daddy will make up.

that I will never again be
deceived and betrayed by another person.

to have great weather
for our garden party in two weeks.

that we retain everything
we've learned forever and ever.

that there's a chocolate
on my pillow for me every night.

that we never cease to be amazed.

that the future Antarctica
will still belong only to the penguins.

that next time I lose
I can be a better sport about it.

that those in power will listen
to the children of the world once in a while.

that the publisher likes
our next book idea.

that love never dies.

that wonders never end.

that imagination conquers boredom.

that my opinion counts too.

that there were more silly people.

that no more trees die.

that we never lose faith
in the power of shooting stars.

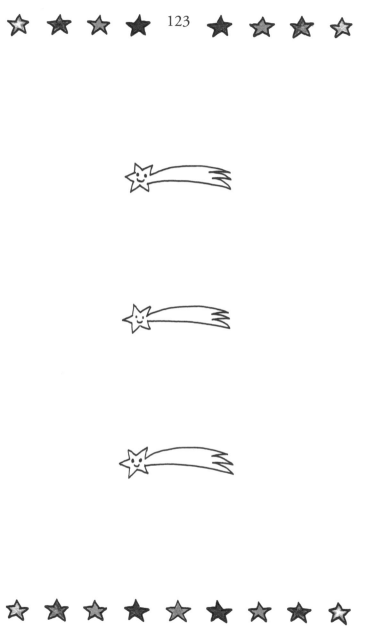

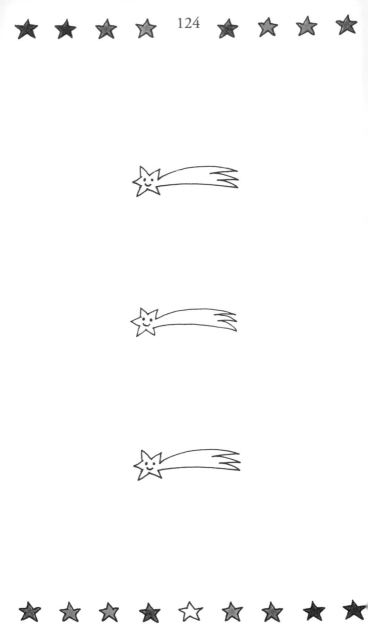

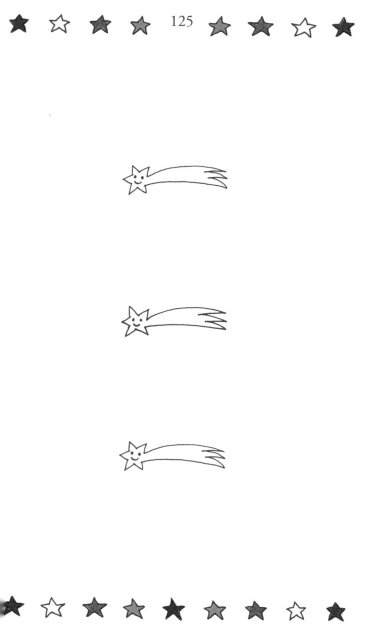

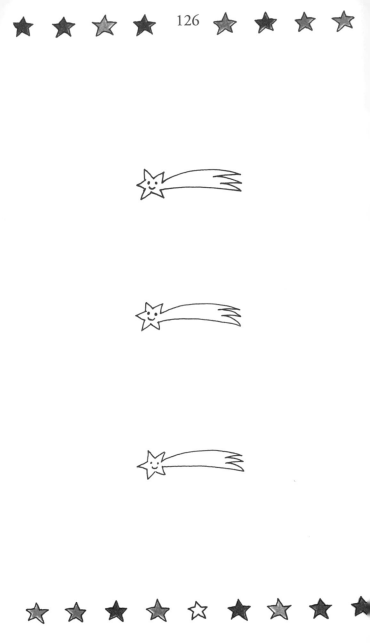

We'd like to thank

the schoolchildren of Vettelschloss and St. Katharinen elementary schools in Westerwald for invaluable inspiration and wonderfully crazy wishes;

the 1992 class of the Oskar-von-Millar-Gymnasium in Munich for critical scrutiny;

Rolf Heyne, Hans-Peter Übleis, and Ria Lottermoser for wishing along with us;

everybody at Abbeville Press for their commitment to this book;

Laura Lindgren for her excellent English translation;

Jutta Peschke for impeccably transcribing all the wishes in this book.

Cat Geller for the paradise in which these ideas first blossomed;

Fabian and Nikolaus Harmstorf for the nightly talks that led us to the concept of this book;

and our children, because every day they demonstrate the power of wishing before our eyes.

❖ ❖ ❖ ❖ ❖ ❖ ❖